Life on the Farm

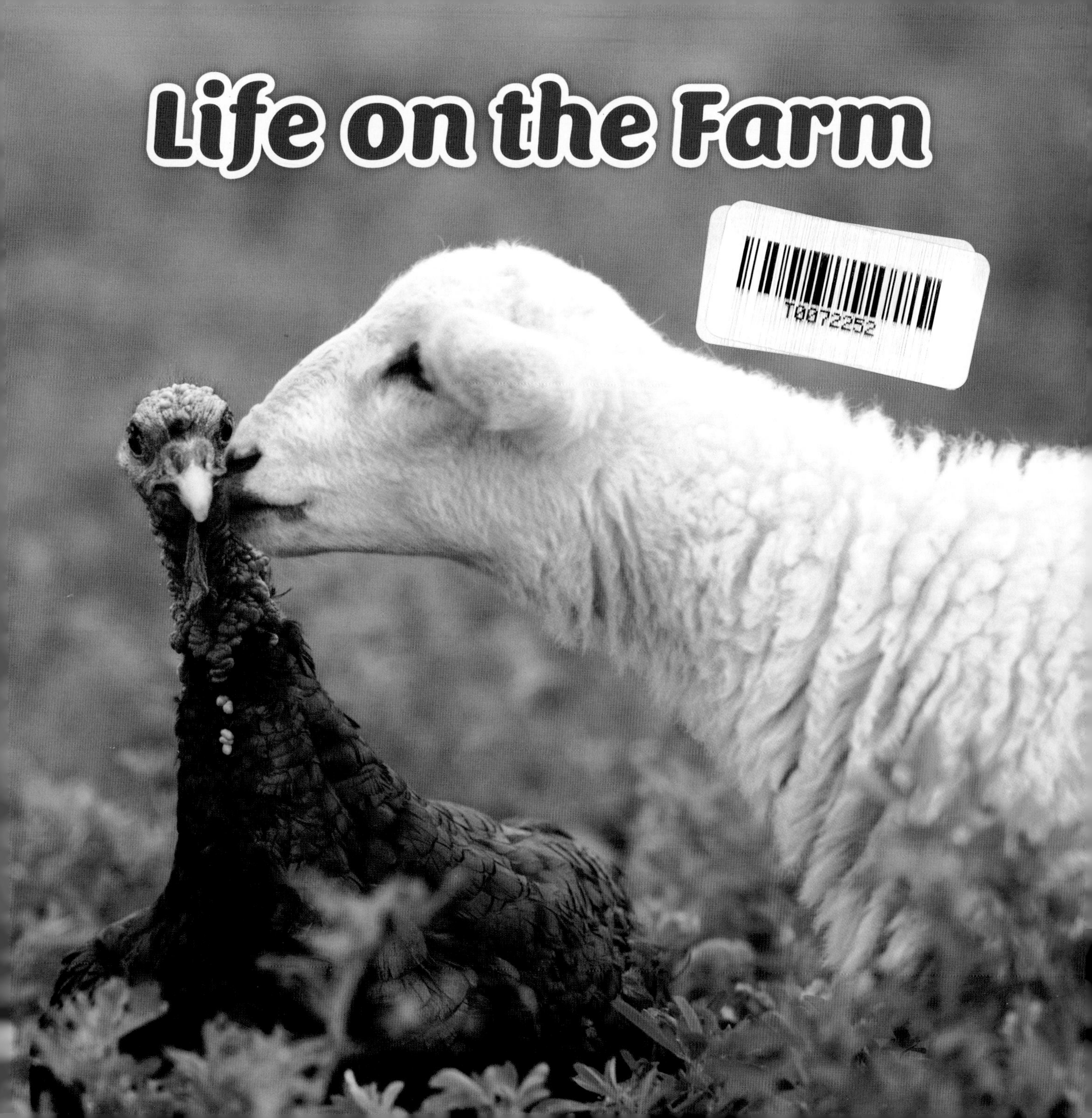

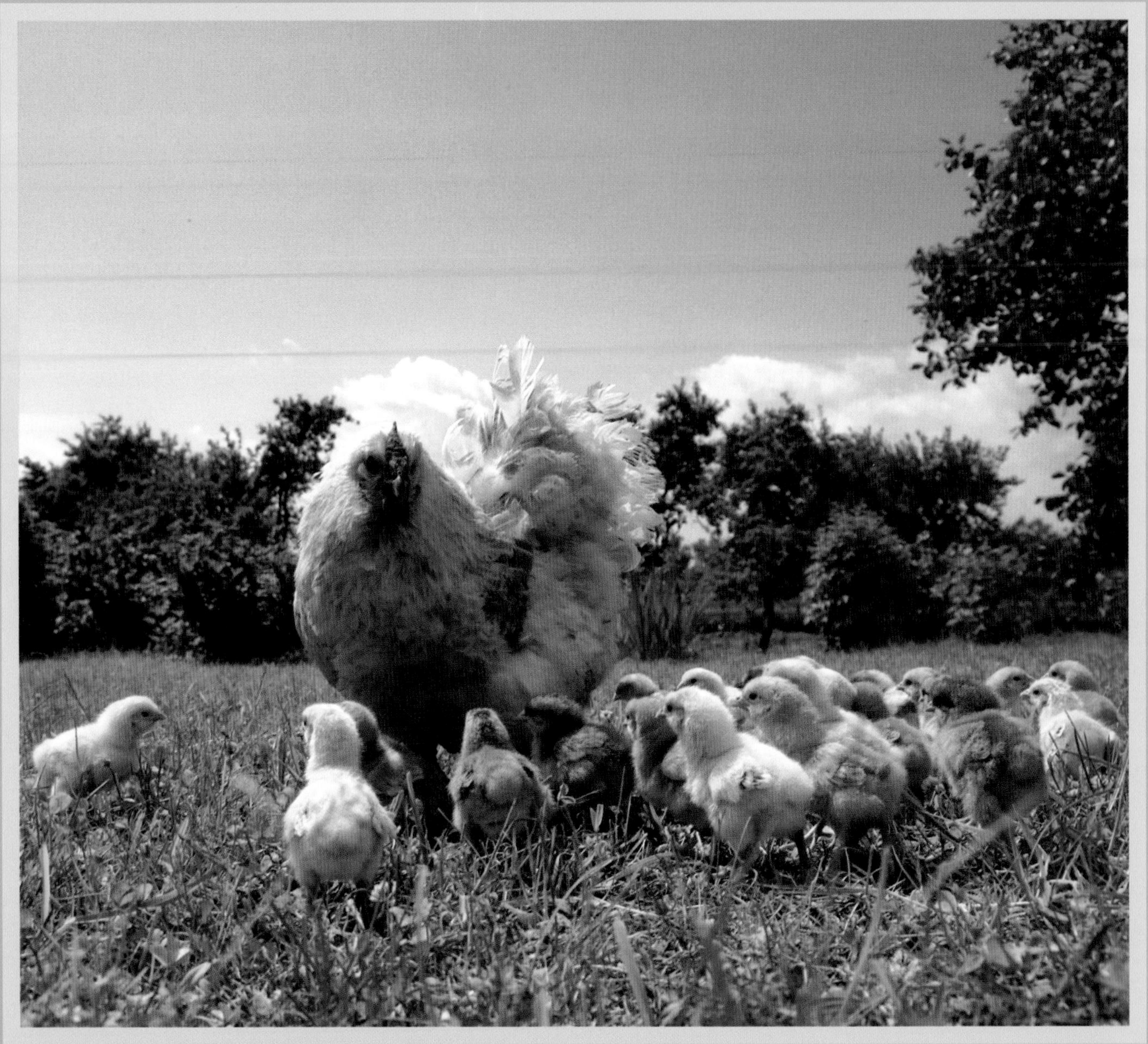

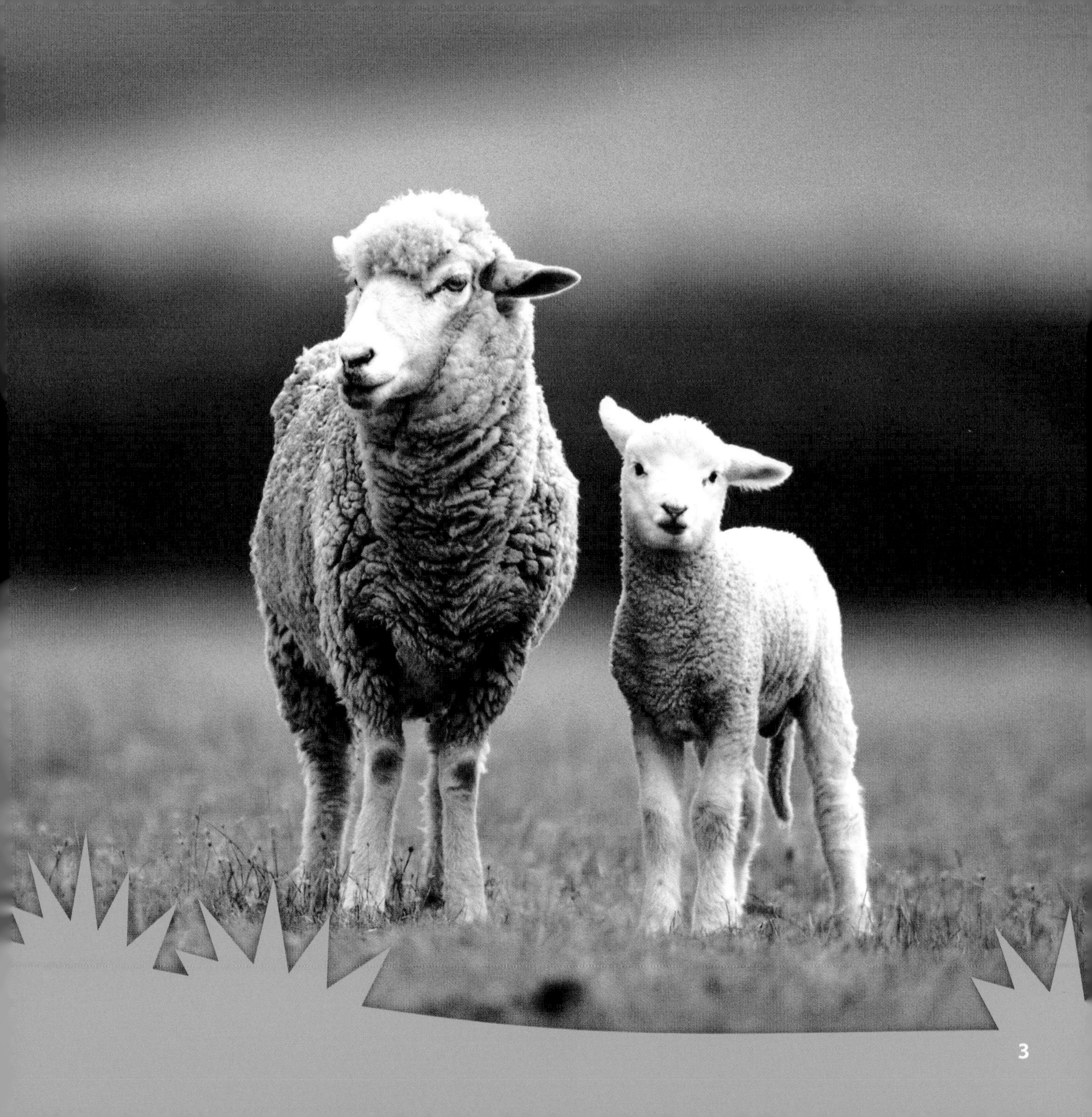

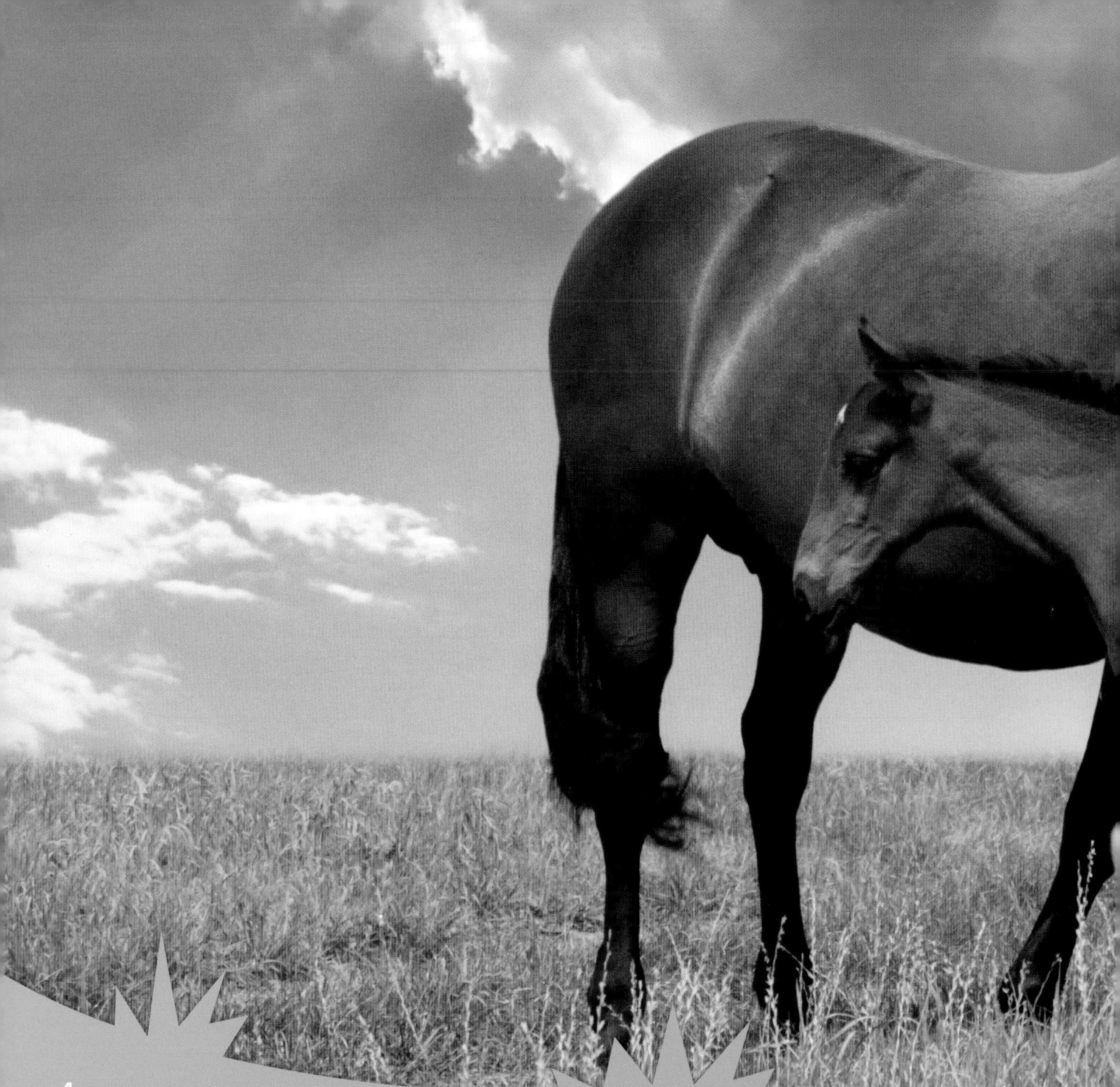

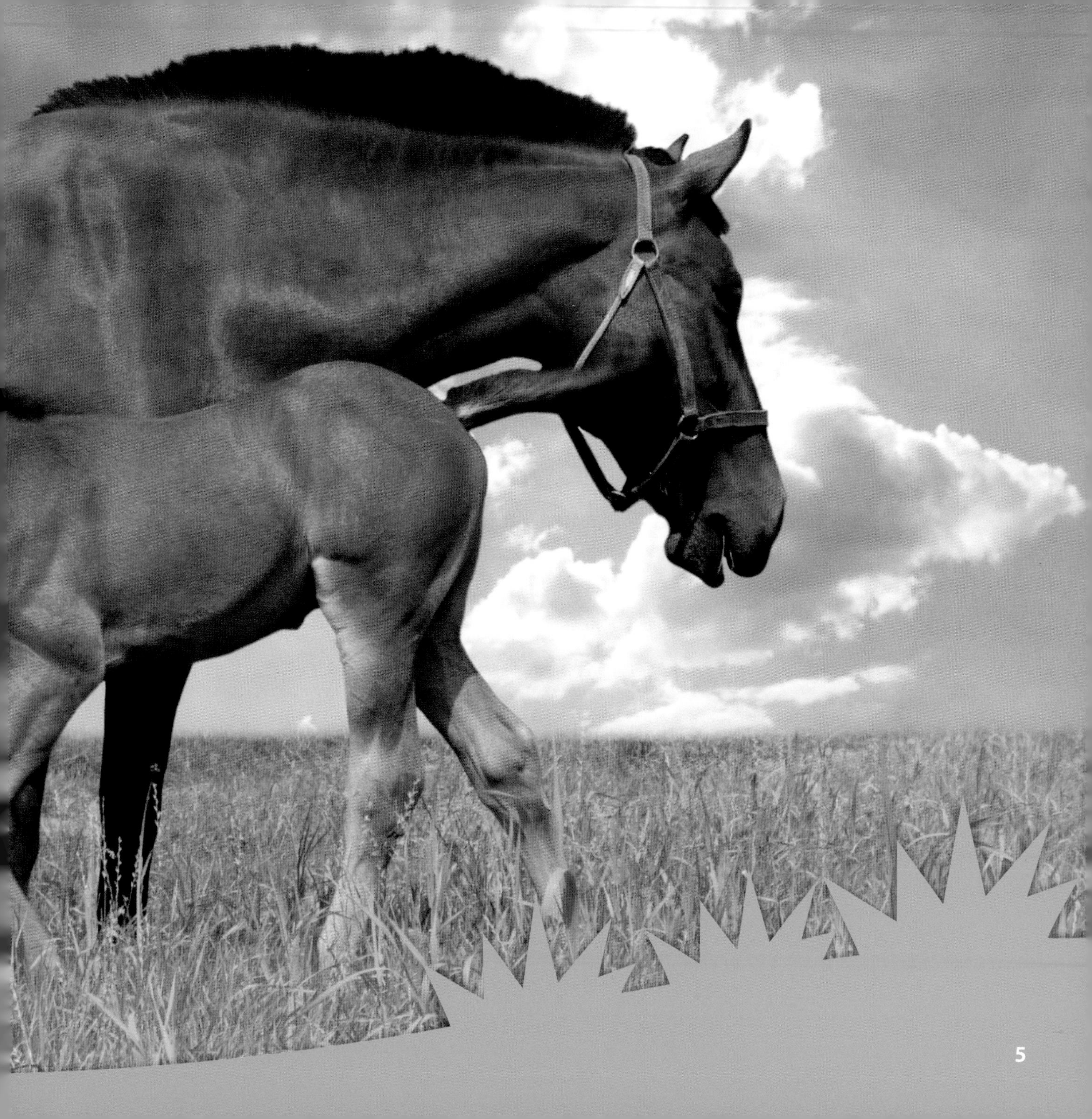

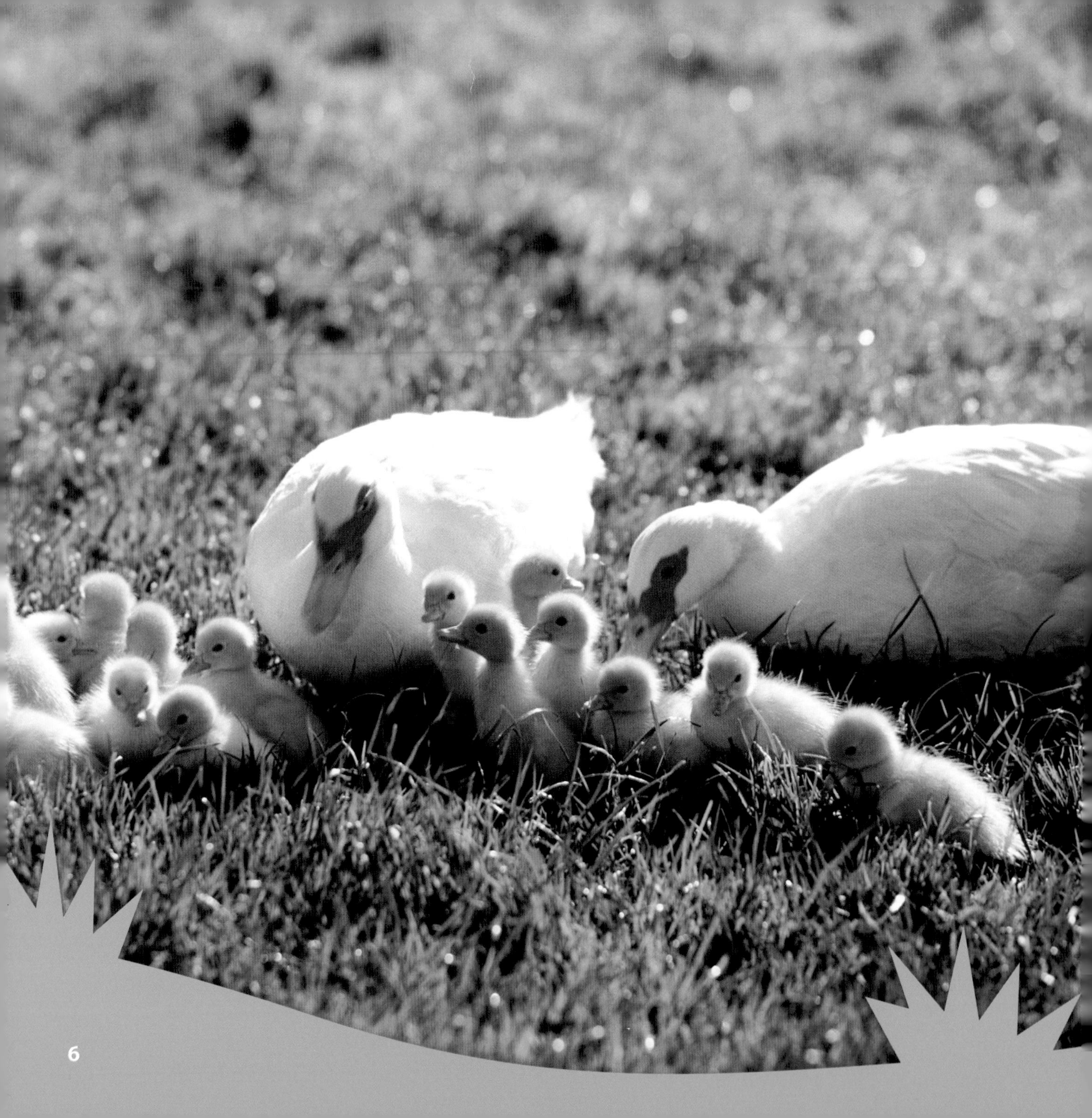

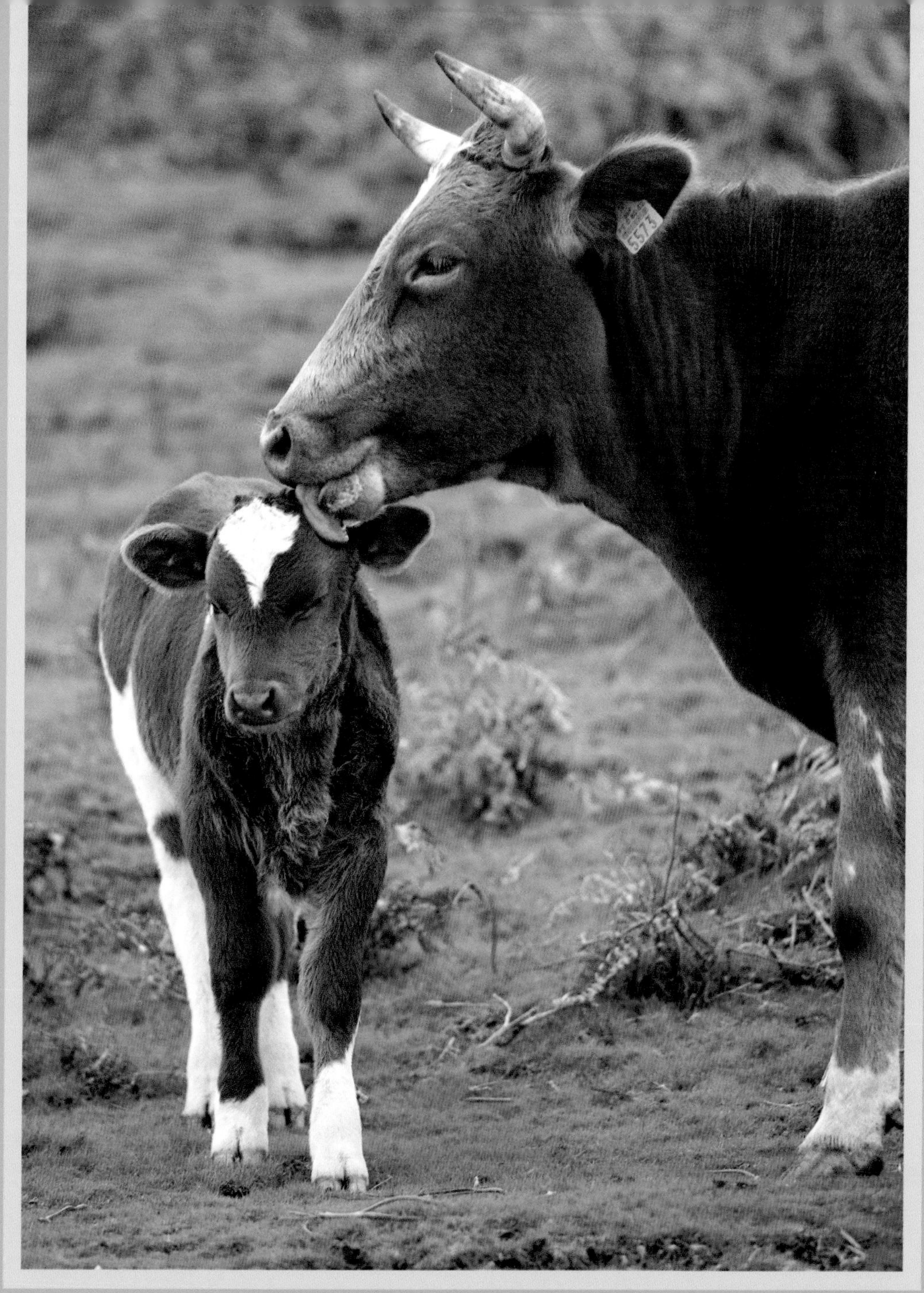
5573

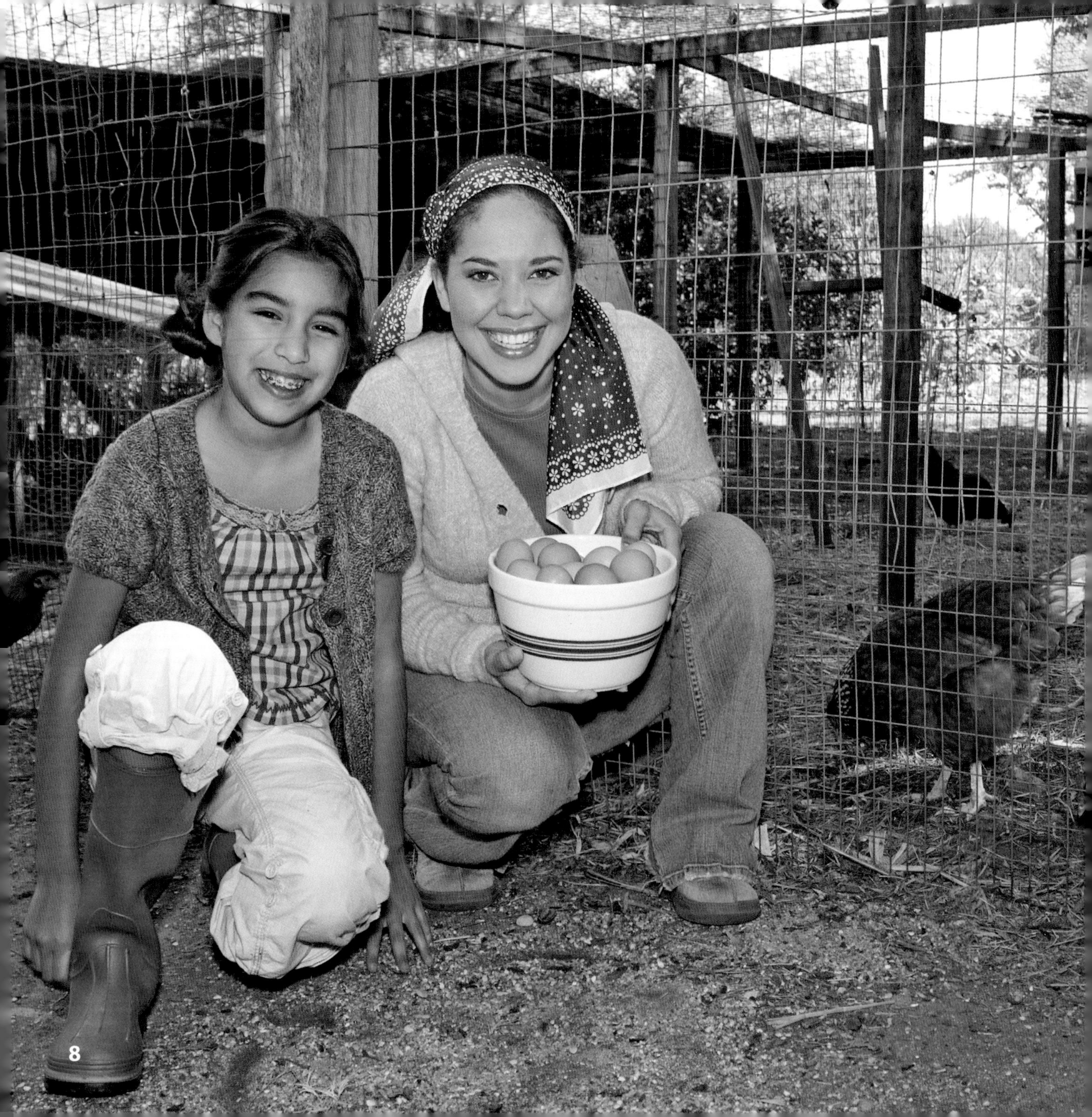